# WHO MADE YOU?

Written by Laurie Colacini Stanton

Illustrated by Mary and James Stanton

Original oil paintings by Frank Colacini

AuthorHouse™
1663 Liberty Drive, Suite 200
Bloomington, IN 47403
www.authorhouse.com
Phone: 1-800-839-8640



First published by AuthorHouse 9/2/2008

ISBN: 978-1-4343-9541-2 (sc)

Library of Congress Control Number: 2008907632

Printed in the United States of America
Bloomington, Indiana

This book is printed on acid-free paper.

This book is dedicated to my Mother and Father
who teach me how to be a good parent,

to my Daughter and Son
who teach me how to be a good person,

and to my Husband
who teaches me to have inner strength
and to have fun!

**WHO** MADE YOU?

DO YOU KNOW **WHO**?

THAT **WHO** MUST BE QUITE PROUD OF YOU!!

THE **WHO** WHO MADE YOU MUST BE GREAT...
YOU'RE NOT TOO EARLY
YOU'RE NOT TOO LATE.

YOU'RE HERE RIGHT NOW,
JUST RIGHT ON TIME....
TO MAKE OUR WORLD BETTER,
TO THINK, DANCE, AND RHYME...

TO LOVE AND TO PLAY,
TO MAKE SPECIAL EACH DAY!!

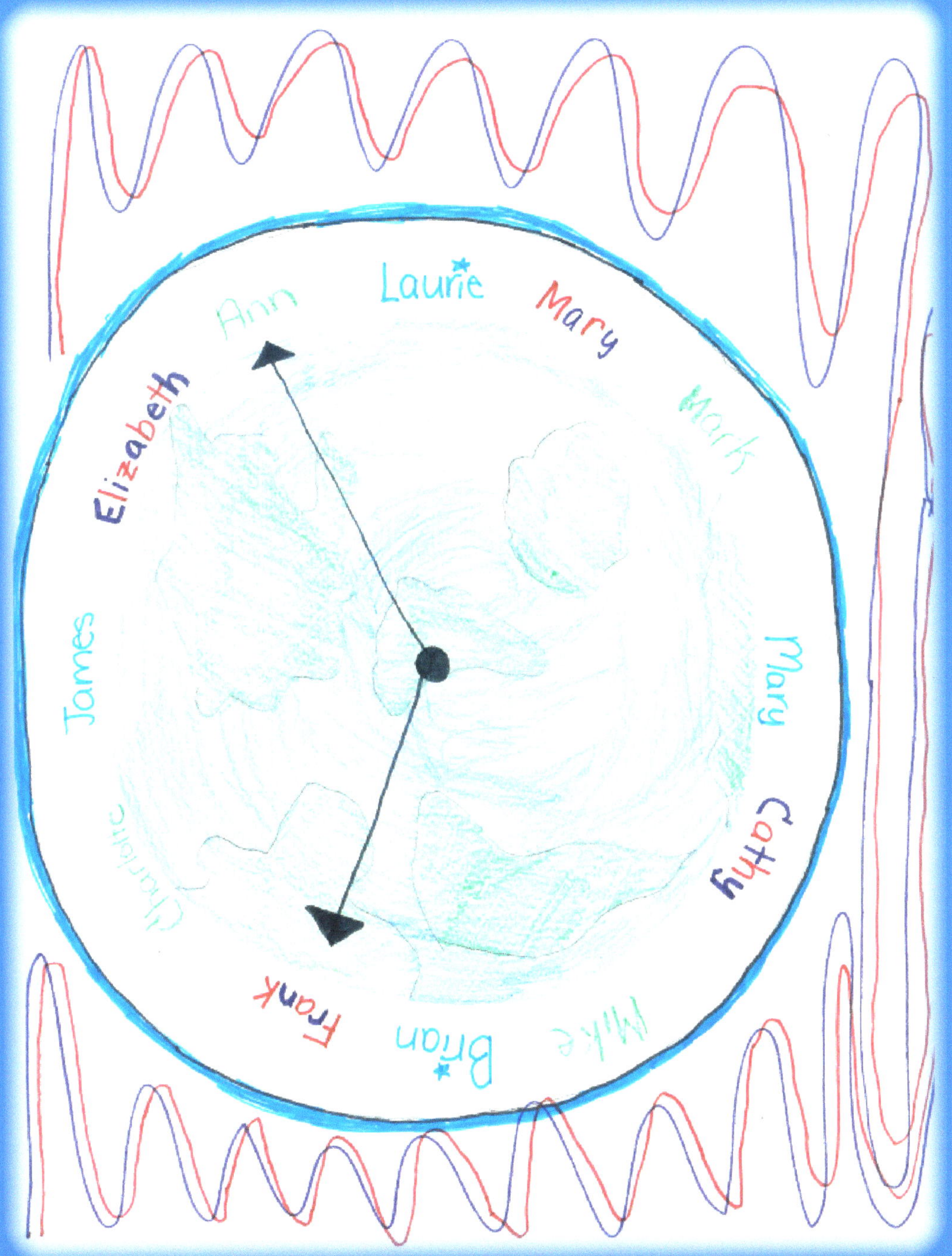

Laurie
Mary
Mark
Mary
Cathy
Mike
Brian
Frank
Charlotte
James
Elizabeth
Ann

THE **WHO** WHO MADE YOU
MUST BE SO KIND!!

LOVING AND CARING
MUST BE ON THEIR MIND!!

NOW THIS **WHO**
WHO MADE YOU....
DID THEY ALSO MAKE ME?

AND WHAT ABOUT HER...
AND HIM...
AND THAT TREE?

AND WHAT ABOUT OCEANS,
MUSIC,
AND ART?

THE **WHO** WHO MADE ALL OF THIS
SURELY IS SMART!!

Wow! you're smart

THIS **WHO** MUST WANT US TO SHARE ALL THAT THEY MADE....
THE SEA AND THE AIR,
THE SUN AND THE SHADE,
THE EARTH AND THE STARS,
AND THE MOONBEAMS THAT GLOW,
THE ROCKS AND THE GRASS,
AND THE RIVERS THAT FLOW.

IF THE WHO WHO MADE ALL OF THIS
AND ALL OF US TOO....
PUT US ALL HERE TOGETHER NOW
WHAT SHOULD WE DO?

PERHAPS LOVE EACH OTHER
AND ALL THE THINGS THAT ARE HERE....
PERHAPS HELP EACH OTHER
AND HOLD THESE THINGS VERY DEAR.

Who Made you

SO WHEN YOU MEET SOMEONE
WHO IS DIFFERENT AND NEW....

REMEMBER WHO MADE THEM....
THE SAME **WHO** WHO MADE YOU!!!!

Im new here
want to Play?
ok letsgo

F. Colacini '05

Laurie Colacini Stanton is originally from Westchester County, New York. Having been raised by a loving family in the serene Hudson River valley, she has a great appreciation for the beauty of nature. Now residing in Florida with her own wonderful family, Laurie aspires to help parents and children embrace the beauty of childhood.

www.ingramcontent.com/pod-product-compliance
Ingram Content Group UK Ltd.
Pitfield, Milton Keynes, MK11 3LW, UK
UKHW060116300726
14090UKWH00002B/218
*9781434395412*